FIT FOR

A MANUAL FOR FIREFIGHTERS.

HEALING FROM WORK RELATED TRAUMA, RESTORING PERSONAL RELATIONSHIPS, AND THRIVING AT HOME

Peter Salerno, PsyD

For Firefighters and their families

Table of Contents

About the Author

Peter Salerno, Psy.D., LMFT, is a licensed psychotherapist and award- winning author residing in Southern California, who holds a doctoral degree in psychology, a master's degree in clinical psychology, and a bachelor's degree in English literature. Dr. Salerno is a trauma specialist who utilizes evidence-based, attachment-oriented approaches to promote healing and self-empowerment. He works with individuals of all ages, couples, and families in private practice. Dr. Salerno grew up in a firefighter family. His father is a retired fire captain, and his brother is a firefighter the union president of his department. Dr. Salerno is dedicated to healing those who serve and their family members.

Website: drpetersalerno.com
Email: <u>peter@drpetersalerno.com</u>
Instagram: @drpetersalerno

INTRODUCTION

This Book and You

This book is about the reality of work-related trauma exposure and how trauma impacts every aspect of your life both on and off duty.

Every firefighter is a trauma survivor. I know this not only because I am a trauma specialist by trade, but because I am the son of a fire captain and the younger brother of a firefighter. You could say I grew up in a "domestic" firehouse of sorts. I saw the impact that the job had on both my father and my older brother, and how it changed them in ways nobody in our family would have ever expected.

What exactly is trauma? Trauma is caused by an overwhelming response to actual or perceived threat in our nervous system (Gentry, 2021). Trauma signs can range from a moderate level of anxiety to severe debilitation, the latter causing many firefighters to wonder whether they are "permanently damaged" or "going crazy." A fire engineer I worked with in therapy described the flooding of his nervous system as becoming *vapor locked.*

"I have to down a case of beers just to feel normal," he confessed to me. Given the research on trauma, not only is his attempt at self-medicating not surprising, but his response made perfect sense to me as a trauma professional. And therein lies the problem. The trauma responses you as a firefighter consistently experience to can render you vulnerable to all kinds of negative consequences and may result in you believing (falsely) that you are powerless, defective, or even to blame for the way you think and feel after direct exposure to on-duty critical incidents or medical emergencies.

Firefighters exposed to critical incidents experience clinically identifiable mental and physical signs of being traumatized. These can arise immediately following an incident or have a delayed onset, which means the signs can develop much later, even years after an event has taken place.

"I can't stop crying," a fire captain told me as he shifted on the couch, unable to get comfortable. "I cry about everything...*everything*. I start crying when I'm watching TV and a stupid commercial comes on, or when I see someone walking their dog, or when I close my eyes and try to sleep. I don't know what's wrong with me. I'm so weak. That's what it is. I'm so weak."

This fire captain is definitely not weak. But no matter how many times I've told him his crying bouts are a completely normal and adaptive response to chronic overwhelming trauma exposure, he shakes his head. He has convinced himself that there is something "wrong" with him and that he has become weak. I finally sent him home with an advance copy of this book, and he called to tell me he felt much better "now that things made sense."

My hope is that the information in this book helps to normalize whatever experiences you may be going through so you can trust that you are reacting to your job in an anticipated way. There truly is help and support out there for you that actually works. You just need to seek it out, and it will be there for you when you're ready.

Basically, the purpose of this book is to help you to make sense of things. To make sense of what you're experiencing. To help you to understand and recognize signs of chronic stress, and to give you the tools not just to "cope" but to heal yourself. Not only will this help you to better do your job, but your off-duty relationships will benefit greatly as well, and you will enjoy your time off.

A Few Words about an Old-School Mindset

The notion of the "good old boys' club" in the workplace, one that operates under old-school notions of camaraderie and pride and a "suck it up" mentality, is finally beginning to fade out, thanks to the fire service evolving and adapting. These old schoolers used to spout things like, "if you need any time off related to stress rather than physical injury, you might as well just quit because you can't handle it." This myth has permeated the fire service since its inception even though the ignorance and negligence of this old way of viewing stress has resulted in the deaths of many of your own. Because members of this club have promoted the dangerous myth that reactions to work-related stress and trauma are signs of weakness, those in need of help sometimes don't seek it.

I have worked with and continue to work with countless firefighters who have told me the same story: they waited way too long to come to see me for help because word around the department was that if they reveal that they are experiencing stress, not only will this damage their reputation, but it's likely that they will be told to quit their job—to literally walk away from their livelihood or risk being fired. This is appalling, but given that there are still out of step old-schoolers in supervisory roles in the fire service, it's unfortunately understandable.

In some agencies, firefighters have gone to their supervisors when they are concerned about the wellbeing of somebody on their crew—are even worried that someone might take their own life. Too many supervisors have brusquely responded that the person in trouble needs to quit if they can't handle the job. Every organization has its blind spot, but the notion that firefighters don't need to seek help for their trauma exposure because of the outdated belief that seeking professional help is a sign of weakness has literally resulted in premature deaths from trauma-induced heart attacks, strokes, and even suicide.

This dangerous misconception has been promoted by supervisors and personnel who either don't know or don't care to know how traumatic stress affects anatomy and physiology. The saddest part about this is that reactions to traumatic stress have nothing to do with mental health, at least in the way "mental health" is commonly understood. Somebody who is experiencing posttraumatic stress is actually having a very adaptive and normal response.

Yes, glorified fraternities still exist in the fire service, but fortunately, they are moving toward extinction. The old-schoolers of the fire service are finally being weeded out, and many more lives will be spared and repaired because of this.

A Brief Introduction to Trauma

Our autonomic nervous system is brilliantly designed to activate a response that allows us to detect threats so that we can protect ourselves and survive. This system works *for* us, not against us. Every time you go on a call your body naturally releases the chemicals necessary to perform the task at hand, and your sympathetic nervous system switches on, as it should.

This is the same thing that happens to animals in the wild when they are being chased by a predator. The main difference between humans and prey animals occurs in the aftermath of the threat. When the threat is no longer present for the animal, its nervous system naturally reverts to "rest and digest" or to the parasympathetic mode. Because of this, animals don't develop trauma responses after the fact. Animals simply move on until the next threatening event takes place, and if they are fortunate enough to survive that one too, they rest and digest again, and so on.

Why isn't it the same for humans? Because traumas are more *personal* in nature for humans than they are for animals, so humans view trauma much differently. A zebra doesn't take it personally when a lion chases them with the intention of mauling them to death. After the near-death experience, the zebra merely returns to the herd to graze. What happened is simply a fact of nature—nothing personal. Prey animals live in the present moment all the time. In contrast, humans live in the past much of the time. This is because the brain recycles and repeats old thoughts over and over. Unless we introduce new thoughts intentionally into our brain, we are condemned to repeat the thoughts from the past.

When your brain and body repeat trauma memories, it is because those memories are literally stuck in your brain and remain unprocessed (Shapiro, 2018). They need to be moved from your memory "inbox" to your memory "archive" file. The treatment required to fix this is simple; it's a tactical method that has given countless firefighters and first responders their lives back. It restores clarity of thought, physical health, repairs personal relationships, and sets you free to enjoy your time off and your retirement.

This, and other solutions, will be outlined within this book. The truth is that while it may not seem so right now, the vast majority of what you experience from trauma exposure can be very easily overcome in very little time.

Chapter One

SIGNS OF TRAUMA

Reliving a Past Event in the Present Moment

Reliving a past event in the present moment is a common indicator of trauma. You may find yourself ruminating over a particular call or several calls, whether recent or from early in your career. Or you might be subjected to memories popping into your mind unexpectedly and at seemingly random times. These are known as flashbacks. You can also experience reliving an event while you sleep in the form of nightmares.

The experience of unsettling physiological reactions in your body is always present in trauma. All five of your senses can trigger the reliving of a disturbing memory, depending on how the information entered your brain and nervous system at the time of the incident. For example, while off-duty you might unthinkingly move your hands in a way that mirrors a similar movement or gesture you made during a distressing call. That simple hand movement alone can transport you back to the call in both your mind and your body. Or you might see blood or smell smoke causing memories of disturbing calls related to those elements to come flooding back to you. You might feel as if you are reliving that particular call all over again in the present moment.

I worked with a probationary firefighter who had responded to a tragic call where an infant had drowned. In the aftermath of this traumatic event, merely gazing at her own eighteen-month-old daughter triggered flashbacks. She told me her eyes would start to tear up and she would experience tremendous guilt when she was even in the same room as her own child. She came to me desperate and confused. I reassured her that while a flashback is a horrible thing to experience, it is also completely normal after going on a call of that nature. Flashbacks can also be successfully eliminated with the right intervention.

Avoidance Strategies

Human beings have natural defense mechanisms, and every human defense mechanism involves some degree of avoidance. As human beings, we instinctively tend to avoid pain and discomfort (Gerson, 2021). Avoidance can range from refusing to go to certain places, to purposely avoiding certain people or certain situations, to attempting to bury or suppress memories, to completely tuning out or "dissociating" as an attempt to avoid reliving a traumatic incident.

Dissociation is the experience of feeling detached from your own conscious awareness or even your own body (DSM 5). It can make you feel like you are "not real" or like the world around you isn't real. More severe experiences of dissociation can result in a complete tuning out, as if you're "here but not here." Because of this, dissociation can trigger humiliation or confusion (DSM-5).

Many firefighters I work with dissociate quite regularly and don't even realize it. If someone tries to get your attention while you are in a state of dissociation, it can be quite startling. Dissociation is really just your brain and your body's way of protecting itself from reliving overwhelming traumatic events, and it can be worked through, but to do so requires a willingness to try something new.

A battalion chief I worked with was triggered by a difficult question I had asked him during one of our sessions, and I witnessed him fall into a dissociative state right before my eyes. His disorientation was so severe, he asked me how he got to my office. His actual words were: "how did I get here, and who are you?" He looked terrified and confused. He couldn't recall driving himself to our appointment because he literally entered into an alternate state as a means of protection from the trauma that was triggered.

Activation and Hyperarousal

Dangerous situations naturally activate your autonomic nervous system. After experiencing a trauma, however, activation can persist for an indefinite amount of time, even long after the traumatic event is over. Reminders of the trauma can activate a threat response such as fear or anxiety, and it can seem like the fear or the anxiety come from out of nowhere because it is difficult to trace trauma signs back to the original event when you're still actively perceiving a threat. This seemingly blindsiding fear or anxiety can sometimes escalate to full-blown panic attacks.

Panic attacks are characterized by a feeling of intense fear or distress that seemingly comes out of nowhere (DSM-5). Panic attacks can abruptly come on even when you think you are in a calm state. Signs of a panic attack include: heart palpitations, sweating, trembling or shaking, shortness of breath or a feeling of being suffocated, feelings of choking, chest pain or discomfort, nausea or abdominal distress, dizziness, lightheadedness, chills or heat sensations, numbness or tingling sensations, dissociation, fear of losing control, fear of "going crazy," and fear of dying (DSM-5).

In addition to experiencing anxiety or panic, you may also find yourself quick to anger or "on edge" on a regular basis. You may find it hard to concentrate. You may seem overly aware of your surroundings. Difficulty sleeping comes with the territory of being a firefighter, but sleep disturbances can be exacerbated by chronic stress. You may be constantly on high alert even when you are fatigued. It is quite taxing to be exhausted and fully alert at the same time.

Negative Thoughts and Beliefs

Shifts in thoughts and beliefs are very common after experiencing traumatic stress. As kids, we develop beliefs and perceptions about how we understand ourselves, others, and the world around us. It is common, however, for these beliefs to change after experiencing traumatic events. For example, after chronic trauma exposure, many firefighters report that they start to believe the world is nothing more than a bleak and dangerous place void of any joy or hope. Because of this, many firefighters find it hard to trust others. Some even stop seeing the point of living and struggle to find meaning in life after trauma exposure. Too many come to believe that they are going to live the rest of their lives as if they are "broken" or "hardened" beyond repair. Many also begin questioning long-held beliefs about their spirituality and the nature of existence. Some firefighters I have worked with blame themselves not only for the way they feel after the traumatic events they've experienced, but for the actual events themselves.

Intense Reactivity

Trauma can activate very strong reactions of anger, irritability, guilt, shame, grief, confusion, worry, and profound sadness. Others may experience you as numb or withdrawn.

Firefighters will often tell me that they want to work on eliminating or at least reducing a specific reaction such as frequent outbursts of anger, but a particular reaction or behavior is rarely the root of the problem. Again, an intense reaction to a traumatic event is just one of many signs that you have been traumatized.

Let's say you're angry: your anger is not the problem. The threat response that accompanies the anger is the actual problem (Gentry, 2021). Once you realize this, it will bring you tremendous relief because you will understand that there's nothing wrong with you personally; what's wrong is that your nervous system is still perceiving threat when there is no actual danger.

Self-Destructive Behaviors

Trauma can lead to excessive and impulsive behaviors that were uncharacteristic of you before the trauma occurred. These can include forms of self-medicating, such as drinking, drug use, smoking and using tobacco and cannabis products, as well as gambling, excessive spending, excessive exercise, excessive television watching, excessive use of your phone for unimportant things, excessive zoning out, excessive or inappropriate sexual activity including infidelity/extramarital affairs, excessive pornography viewing, detachment from family members, self-sabotaging behaviors, and excessive activity scheduling to avoid down time and keep busy, among other things.

I'm being careful here by saying that trauma can *lead* to these behaviors, because trauma itself cannot make anyone do anything. Trauma can highly influence your behaviors on a non-conscious level because trauma hijacks your autonomic nervous system and the limbic region (the emotional center of your brain), which can lead you to act out of character until you realize you are not in any danger and until you learn how to interrupt the threat response in your body. You can determine if you're acting out of character quite simply: if you have begun to behave in ways that are not typical of you, and you experience guilt, shame, or remorse, then you know you are acting out of character.

When it comes to self-destructive behaviors, I want to emphasize that there is a major difference between an explanation and an excuse. When I work with firefighters and their spouses, significant others, or close family members and when I explain what trauma does to the nervous system, I am often met with defensiveness on the part of the spouse, partner, or family member because it's tempting to interpret explanations of the effects of trauma as excuses for inappropriate behavior. As stated before, I am the son of a fire captain and the brother of a firefighter, so I am personally well-versed on the impact that work-related trauma in the fire service has on a firefighter's personal and family relationships. Because of this, I would never justify a behavior that causes pain or suffering for someone related to a firefighter. Let me be clear: work-related trauma exposure can provide an *explanation* for why you may be more tempted to engage in behaviors that are inconsistent with your character, but it doesn't excuse behaviors that are harmful to yourself or to others.

If you find you are acting out of character, it is really important to seek help, especially if you have other people depending on you in your personal life. If you don't seek help or practice the self-help techniques in this book regularly, you could potentially rupture relationships in ways that might be difficult or even impossible to repair. As human beings, when we don't allow ourselves to think and feel things, we leave ourselves no other choice but to act out. While it is completely normal to be tempted to act out of character when you are perceiving threat after a trauma, it is in your best interest to be accountable for yourself and considerate of your loved ones by taking your path to healing seriously.

Chapter Two

The Unpredictability of Trauma

As a trauma specialist, I am here to tell you that there would be something wrong with you if you *didn't* have an adverse reaction to what you are exposed to while on duty. This is very important to understand and I can't emphasize this enough. It would be *abnormal* if you were not stressed out after work-related critical incidents. If somebody can walk away unscathed from scene after scene of heinous tragedies, I would suspect that this person would have some degree of disorder in their personality functioning. Based on the nature of your job, you *should* be experiencing adverse reactions to critical incidents.

Our mental and physical wellbeing for the most part depends on our ability to recognize patterns and anticipate outcomes (Gerson, 2021). That's how the brain works; it's basically a survival and prediction machine. Typically, we have control over the memories we recall, and we can control when they start and when they stop. But trauma hijacks this ability to the point that we are no longer in control of what we experience because we are still perceiving threat long after the threat is gone. When this happens, we will try to avoid or push certain memories away, and this only makes matters worse over time. Prolonged stress produces prolonged mental and physical consequences and make it seem like threats that have already taken place are still happening and relevant (Shapiro, 2018).

Mental Disorder or Mental Adaptation?

Trauma is not a mental disorder; it is an adaptive response to environmental stimuli. Let me repeat that: trauma is *not* a disorder. It is extremely important for their overall wellbeing that firefighters understand that being traumatized is an adaptive response that comes with the territory of being a firefighter. One way to look at it: it's not "normal" to experience what firefighters experience even one day on duty, but it is very normal for them to have adverse reactions to what they have been exposed to.

It is true that the American Psychiatric Association classifies trauma and stress related responses as "disorders" in the Diagnostic and Statistical Manual of Mental Disorders, 5th Edition. Though the DSM-5 is considered to be the bible in my profession, this doesn't tell the full story. It is my professional assertion—and I've worked with literally thousands of firefighters—that you would most definitely have a disorder if you were *not* affected by what you experience on the job.

Diagnostic Overload

Medical professionals in general medicine and psychiatry as well as mental health practitioners are trained to label their patients with formal diagnoses and prescribe medication or provide referrals for medication evaluations. This is done after collecting "data" on a person and checking off boxes from a list of "criteria." In my view, this data/criteria approach is shortsighted when applied to first responders dealing with critical incident trauma-related ailments.

If you've ever sought professional help in the past, you might have been told that you have one of the more common "disorders" such as:

Posttraumatic Stress "Disorder"
Major Depressive "Disorder"
Bipolar "Disorder"
Generalized Anxiety "Disorder"
Attention Deficit Hyperactivity "Disorder"
Acute Stress "Disorder"
Narcissistic Personality "Disorder"
Borderline Personality "Disorder"

Obsessive-Compulsive "Disorder"

Panic "Disorder"

Let me just say that all of us as human beings can check off boxes that meet some of the criteria for any of these "disorders" because a lot of the criteria overlap and a lot of the criteria, like it or not, just describes the experience of being human.

The problem with diagnoses is that they highlight human conditions and then label these human conditions as defects (Walker, 2013). When you're traumatized, and you're told by a professional that you have "defects," this doesn't do you any good. No wonder so many firefighters wouldn't dream of seeking professional help. Who would want to seek support only to be told that they have a problem or that they are defective? Not me. I expect not you either.

I'm here to tell you that support exists that does not involve shaming, labeling, or "disordering." When firefighters come to my office to see me, I immediately try to lighten the mood and to instill hope. Why else would you come seek help? To commiserate? That doesn't do anything but reinforce the idea that something is wrong, and there's nothing "wrong" with you. Being traumatized is part of the job.

Chapter Three

TRAUMA AND THE BRAIN

Traumatic events literally alter the structure and functioning of the brain and autonomic nervous system. The way memories are stored in the brain affects the way we perceive our environment, the attitudes we have, and the behaviors we exhibit (Shapiro, 2012). The three regions of the brain that are important to memory processing and trauma are the amygdala, the hippocampus, and the thalamus, and these will be explained in detail below (see *Figure 1*).

The Amygdala

You can think of the amygdala as the brain's smoke detector. The word "amygdala" means almond, and there are two of them in our brain. The amygdalae are located in the limbic region, which is the emotional center of the brain. The amygdalae are designed to alert us to potential threats and dangers within our environment. The amygdalae activate the famous "fight or flight" system that causes the thinking part of the brain to shut down so that the body can run on autopilot in order to survive a threat, whether perceived or actual. Unfortunately, traumatic stress can trigger the amygdala to detect a past threat in the present moment, causing the brain to think the threat is still present. Flashbacks and nightmares are essentially memories trapped in the amygdala.

The Hippocampus

The hippocampus identifies important information taken in through the senses and converts that information from short-term memory into long-term memory. Brain activity increases in the hippocampus during sleep. However, when the brain is in threat-detection mode, it blocks traumatic and stressful memories from entering the long-term memory bank, so the hippocampus is unable to do its job properly. Essentially, traumatic memories get left in the brain's "inbox" rather than being "archived," so they don't receive a time and place stamp. Because of this, whenever traumatic memories are triggered or recalled, it can feel like the memory is not something from the past but is actually happening all over again in the present.

The Thalamus

The thalamus shares sensory information with the rest of the brain, whether quickly to the amygdala, which is the threat-detecting part of the brain, or slowly to the cortex, which is the thinking part of the brain (Sweeton, 2019). The thalamus also takes pieces of information and brings them together to form a complete memory with a beginning, middle, and end. During a traumatic event, however, the thalamus shuts down, so information isn't adequately communicated to the cortex. This is why memories of trauma can seem more like fragments or snapshot images rather than a full story. Pieces might even seem like they are missing.

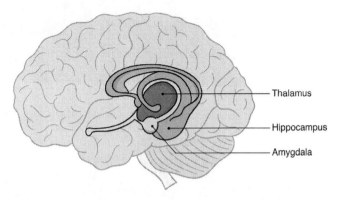

Figure 1. Amygdala, Hippocampus, and Thalamus of the Limbic System. (Image Copyright 2023 Peter Salerno)

Chapter Four

TRAUMA AND THE BODY

When I ask a firefighter during our first session what comes to mind when I say the word "trauma," I almost always get the same response: "physical injury to the brain or body." Anything that renders somebody so physically impaired that they have to seek medical help is typically what we think of as trauma. Traumatic brain injuries, trauma of organ systems, trauma to limbs and other body parts, are some examples.

So, when firefighters say they consider the word "trauma" as referring to a physical injury, I would agree, but not in the way you might think. Traumatic injuries can have a literal physical cause, or they can injure your body by entering through the five senses, putting your

23

nervous system into "fight-or-flight" mode. This is not a mental problem; this is a body problem. Traumatic memories get reactivated by your bodily senses because trauma lives in your autonomic nervous system, and the autonomic nervous system runs throughout your entire body.

In summary, *all* traumas are body problems. You don't have to get into a near fatal car accident and bruise your brain in order to experience significant trauma. You can simply arrive at a call and suffer a traumatic injury after what you experience with your five senses—with what you see, smell, hear, touch, and even taste.

Other Types of Trauma

Work-related trauma can be compounded or exacerbated by other types of trauma that may have occurred before you entered the field of protective services or which may have occurred in your personal life during your career as a firefighter. Cumulative trauma, childhood trauma, vicarious trauma and personal trauma are four variations of trauma that you might recognize.

Cumulative Trauma

Cumulative trauma is the result of a series of traumatic events—one after another—that kept on coming over a period of time. This "stockpiled" trauma is considered complex because it impacts your psychological and physiological systems differently than a single incident trauma like a car accident would, for example.

Childhood Trauma

Childhood trauma consists of any form of verbal, physical, or emotional violations that are too overwhelming for a child at a particular stage of development to process or deal with. This includes physical harm, sexual abuse, verbal criticisms, dismissals, threats, insults, emotional harassment or neglect, among other things. The age at which abuse occurs is relevant because of the varying stages of brain and body development. For example, a verbal threat of physical violence will register differently for a four-year-old versus a seventeen-year-old, but both can still be traumatizing. Traumas experienced before the age of six severely impact psychological and physiological development (Gerson, 2021), but damage sustained can be successfully repaired and healed with professional assistance. It is never too late to heal from the pain of the past.

Indirect exposure by witnessing something distressing also constitutes child abuse. For example, if you are a child of an alcoholic or if you witnessed domestic violence, this indirect traumatic exposure is still abuse if you were under the age of eighteen when it occurred.

Taking inventory of adverse childhood experiences would certainly shed some light on your potential exposure to childhood trauma. The Adverse Childhood Experiences (A.C.E.) questionnaire is a useful tool to determine if you experienced trauma during childhood. You can find an A.C.E. questionnaire free online. This questionnaire can also be provided to you by a mental health professional.

Vicarious Trauma

Vicarious trauma is essentially being traumatized by being in close proximity to someone other than yourself who has been traumatized. This can happen in many ways: hearing a traumatic story, living with a trauma survivor, being a dispatcher and taking calls related to traumatic events, witnessing self-destructive behaviors of a trauma survivor, etc. Though this type of trauma is not experienced "directly," vicarious trauma still needs to be treated like any other form of trauma. Due to the nature of your job and their close proximity to you, your family members and loved ones are likely to experience vicarious trauma to a certain degree. Because of this they, too, may benefit from processing their trauma experience with a professional and may benefit from learning about the self-help exercises in this book.

Personal Trauma

Personal trauma refers to trauma exposure separate from work-related trauma that you may be experiencing at home or in your personal life. This can include the loss of a family member or loved one, relational betrayal/infidelity, emotional neglect, dealing with someone's drug or alcohol addiction, caretaking of a disabled or terminally ill loved one, or experiencing emotional, physical or verbal abuse at home, among other things.

Chapter Five

THE PROBLEM WITH BEING OFF-DUTY

One of the most appealing aspects of pursuing a job in the fire service, at least before one actually works in the fire service, is the schedule. I remember my dad telling me that what appealed to him most was the unconventional work hours. His shift schedule afforded him plenty of opportunities to participate in family functions during the week, including school field trips with the kids. He said that one of the motivating factors for his entering the fire service came about when he had approached another father at my elementary school to ask how he was always able to go on field trips and to volunteer at the school. The man explained that because he was a firefighter, he got to be home not just on some weekends but some weekdays as well.

For a devoted dad, this is an exciting proposition: a job that allows more time with the kids. Although entering the fire service in order to spend more quality time with your family is a noble reason, the reality is not as ideal as most people think. This is something that most firefighters learn very quickly firsthand. Not only are off duty days not very predictable, but off-duty can actually be your worst nightmare for a number of reasons you might not even be aware of.

How so? First off, the impact of trauma you have experienced, whether cumulatively or due to a recent critical incident, can cause the systems of your body to short circuit, rendering you a prisoner of your own body. When this happens, the trauma dwells in every one of your cells, putting you in a constant state of overwhelming stress. You are literally swimming in cortisol and other stress hormones all the time. In this perpetual stress state, the sympathetic nervous system is switched on 24/7, even when you are asleep, so you are never truly at rest, even when you are off duty.

It is true that as a firefighter you are trained and conditioned to operate on very little sleep. So, it's no news to you that your sleep is disturbed whenever you're on duty. Getting woken up in the middle of the night—sometimes several times a night—is the antithesis of a good night's rest. Then, once you're on a call, your body is governed by organ systems that habitually release hormonal "stimulants" such as adrenaline, cortisol, epinephrine, and norepinephrine. These chemicals course through your bloodstream to ensure that you are alert and able to perform necessary tasks while on duty.

The problem is there is no training that I'm aware of in the fire service that teaches you how to turn off the "go" switch once you get home. So, those coveted days of being off-duty can be spent not relaxing or enjoying your time off but in dwelling in a state of toxic stress, in dissociating (feeling detached from your own conscious awareness or even your own body), in dwelling in a state of anger, in getting the urge to self-medicate, in engaging in behaviors that aren't typical of your true character, in sleeping throughout the day, in becoming numb or withdrawn, or even in resenting being home with family—even if that's what you value most in the world.

Essentially, the mind and body of a firefighter are conditioned to operate well <u>only</u> in the context of a highly stressful work environment. But the downside is a heavy price to pay: the mind and body of an off-duty firefighter can become a nightmare. This is obviously not fair; you, as a firefighter, have sacrificed a great deal—both physically and mentally—in order to earn your days off. But still, some of the chief complaints that firefighters have when they come to my office for the first time is that their family life is falling apart. They find they are "unavailable" or disconnected from their partner and their children, if they have children. They're also making decisions that are not in the best interest of their health, whether by coping through self-medication or acting-out behaviors such as partying, over-eating, drinking, gambling, sexual activity, having extramarital affairs, or by only associating with friends while avoiding family. Other chief complaints are anger outbursts, low frustration tolerance, and constant irritability.

Many firefighters I work with actually feel a lot better when they are about to go back to work. Family members, even my own, consistently have reported that "the day before" you go back to work you oftentimes miraculously snap out of your negative mood. This can lead your loved ones to believe that you prefer to be at work. Maybe you do, but it might be that your body prefers it more so than you do.

This sudden onset high-spiritedness isn't so much that you are eager to be away from your family; it has more to do with the physical distraction your autonomic nervous system experiences when it is gearing u to go back to the environment in which it is conditioned to operate. As you might expect, this can be exceedingly difficult for family members to understand. But it's not that *you* dread your home life and desire only to return to the excitement of the danger zone; it's your nervous system that is calling the shots. Of course, there might be other underlying reasons for this dynamic, but this is a major contributor.

Oftentimes the family who is left behind will accuse the firefighter of preferring work and choosing work over the family. This is a sort of chronic misunderstanding that can lead to all kinds of domestic tragedies including divorce or separation, broken families, infidelity, emotional betrayal, domestic violence, etc. You may presume you have fallen out of love with your significant other or you really don't care to be around your kids because domestic life seems much more stressful to firefighters suffering from work-related trauma exposure.

The firefighter may defend choosing work over family by arguing that volunteering for overtime will help the family financially. This may be true, but the real reason is much simpler: it makes more physiological and psychological sense for the body and the mind of a firefighter to be on duty rather than off duty. Sadly, you are probably not even aware of the true reason why you want to go back to work so badly. What's really happening is your body is craving to put into action the chemical state that it's grown accustomed to while you're on duty.

Firefighters who dread the drive home after a shift are actually, and unknowingly, dreading the stress hormones of cortisol and adrenaline coursing through their bloodstream. They aren't craving tragedy so much as craving the opportunity to put those surging stress hormones to good use. Deprived of an environmental stimulus like a fatal car accident or a baby drowning or a teenage suicide or a fire or a drug overdose or a stabbing or shooting to react to, the reactive body is thwarted from too much energy. It's as if the body expects to see an infant dead in the street after being thrust through a windshield in a fatal car wreck, but all it really sees is the normalcy of domestic life.

Basically, your mind and body are geared up for a tragedy, your nervous system is shot, and your brain and body are so sleep deprived that the normalcy of domestic life becomes a nightmare. And life at work, which is the real nightmare, becomes preferred. Ironically, over time, the desire to go back to work fades, and the reverse occurs: you begin to dread going to work. Regardless of which phase you're in, whether it's the desire to work more or the desire to work less, both of these impulses are fueled not by what you desire, but by the fact that your nervous system is flooded.

Why You Can't Sit Still

Almost every firefighter I work with tells me that they prefer to be "on the go." They like always having something to do and they don't like sitting still. You might very well say the same thing. And though this could be due to having an energized nature, I suspect this inclination to always be on the go is a reaction to constantly perceiving threat when there is no actual danger. Unlike animals, firefighters don't "rest and digest" when the life-threatening action stops. Your nervous system is always in sympathetic mode, even when you're off-duty. The truth is that being on the go or being active is typically not a personality trait so much as it is a conditioned behavior. People who have been exposed to trauma typically have a very difficult time sitting still and doing nothing because their muscles are involuntarily constricted when they should be relaxed. Involuntary muscle constriction produces chronic stress in the body (Gentry, 2021). As ridiculously simple as this may sound, if you relax the muscles in your body, stress and anxiety cannot exist. Stress and anxiety can only exist when your muscles are tense, so if the muscles in your body are relaxed, it is literally *impossible* to be stressed or anxious

(Gentry, 2021). Stress is a body problem, not a mental problem. I provide a list of self-help techniques to reduce muscle tension in a later chapter.

Mental Health is Physical Health

A career in the fire service wreaks havoc on your autonomic nervous system. The autonomic nervous system is designed to work for you on the job, but you need to be able to turn it off when you're not on duty. Odds are you have never been taught how to do this. It is a good thing to be intentionally cautious and vigilant while on duty; however, your body rebels against your domestic life because it doesn't know what to do with itself while you're off duty. Many firefighters actually sustain damage to their nerve cells after decades on the job; and this damage doesn't dissipate once they retire. Too often, literally weeks or months into retirement firefighters suffer a heart attack or stroke just when they were about to enjoy their freedom after a life dedicated to the fire service. This is also one of the reasons why suicide rates are exceedingly high after retirement. But such tragic outcomes are not inevitable. Trauma-informed therapy has been shown to restore physical health, that is, to recalibrate your autonomic nervous system so that you will be fit for off-duty.

Trauma-Informed Therapy is the solution that will save your life and make you fit for your off-duty existence. The next section tells you what you need to know about getting help.

Chapter Six

SEEKING ASSISTANCE

The decision to seek out help, while it may be difficult, will give you your life back. You deserve a fulfilling life after dedicating so much of your time entrenched in living nightmares while on duty. Most firefighters are amazed at how many "invisible" behaviors and tendencies they've adopted in response to life on duty have transferred to their off-duty existence. But the true amazement will come at how free and light you will feel and how much you will look forward to spending time with those whom you love—at how you can actually be present in the moment while at home.

Restoring and Repairing Off-Duty Personal Relationships

Trauma exposure from work-related critical incidents can render you unable to feel safe and secure in close relationships, including those with significant others, and if you are a parent, even with your own children (Parnell, 2013). While vacations and material gifts are great to have and should be enjoyed during your off-duty time, they do not fix relationships. I remember my dad being so irritable on our river trips as a kid, back then I almost wished he drank like the other dads so he could have relaxed and enjoyed his time off. Turns out my dad was so tense because he was instinctively perceiving threat even on vacation where there was no threat.

Here is an example of how seemingly small communication avoidance can leave a serious lasting impression and create more detachment at home. A civilian client of mine, the wife of a firefighter, shared this story:

"My husband would come home and before saying hello to me or even acknowledging the kids, he'd plug in the vacuum and start vigorously running it throughout the entire house. The thing is, knowing he'd be home in the morning, I would always vacuum the entire house the night before, and I always keep a clean house. When I would see him do this, it made me feel like my cleaning wasn't good enough. It made me feel horrible. Then, when he finishes vacuuming, he goes out and washes his truck. It's like he walks in the house and demonstrates I'm not doing enough while he's away, before he removes himself from the family. In the early evening he falls asleep in front of the TV. It's like he's not even home. He might as well be at work. This has been going on for ten years. Nothing I do is seems good enough."

For relationships to be healthy off-duty, an understanding of the impact of trauma is necessary not only for you as a firefighter, but for your loved ones as well. Your loved ones need to know what happens to your nervous system while you are at work, and it would be a tremendous help to them to learn how your keyed-up nervous system affects how you relate to everyone and everything outside of work. This requires the use of words, not actions, like it or not. You don't have to go into details about the critical incidents you witness regularly, but you do have to develop new ways of communicating with those you love so they can better understand you.

A paramedic I worked with shared this story: "My wife is very affectionate, but her need for physical contact has started to irritate me within the last few years. When I'm home and we walk the dog, she's always trying to hold my hand. Because I get so agitated by this, I think I need some more alone time when I'm off."

After participating in trauma-informed therapy and learning how to shut off the "fight-or-flight" switch, this paramedic came to the realization that he had been pushing his wife away for years out of fear of losing her. The job was impacting him so much that he began slowly detaching from the person he loved most. He hadn't realized the trauma he'd experienced at work, and in particular the tragedies he'd witnessed which featured the loss of family members, had impacted his personal life so severely. After a few sessions together, I suggested he write a letter to his wife explaining what he now understood about himself. He also expressed his deep love for her and outlined all he was doing to turn things around. He was more than willing to do this after therapy because he felt so much better—more like himself again.

He sent me an email a few months later telling me that he had gotten his life and his marriage back on track, and that they were going to have a baby soon. That felt good to read.

Trauma-Informed Therapy: A Simple, Life Saving Solution to Complex, Life-Threatening Problems

Trauma-informed therapy is essential for healing from work-related trauma exposure. You're never going to "snap out of it," and it won't get better when you retire, so like it or not, you do need assistance if you want to be free from the impact of trauma.

Traditional talk therapy is helpful but not effective on its own for individuals with a history of trauma exposure (Greenwald, 2013). Traumatic experiences and memories can be isolated in the brain in a way that remain inaccessible when simply talking about them (Greenwald, 2013; Shapiro, 2018).

Because trauma can cause an individual to become "stuck" in the time when the traumatic event occurred, in order to alleviate what is blocking the person from moving forward, it is essential to resolve the conflict that is contributing to the blockage. But there are positive steps you can take to repair your relationships even before undergoing trauma-informed therapy.

Be Vulnerable by Communicating How You Feel. Family members don't really know what they are getting themselves into no matter how much they think they know about the fire service. It's up to you to sit down with your loved ones, no matter how uncomfortable this might be, and share the information from this book and other resources regarding how trauma has impacted you and how you believe it may have impacted them by virtue of being close to you. It is essential that you communicate what you have experienced within yourself—particularly changes you have witnessed—as a result of the job. Reassure your loved ones that they are not the cause of the changes within you.

Be Vulnerable by Admitting the Need for Help. It takes a lot of courage to admit when you need assistance. Just as you rely on your crew at work, you need to start relying on your loved ones for domestic support. Talk to them about trauma-informed therapy and ask them to support you in your decision to seek professional assistance. Let them know that partner and family support during trauma work increases the capacity for healing and speeds up the process of resolution, so their participation will be an essential part of the process. Lastly, inform them about vicarious trauma and let them know help is available for them too.

Be Vulnerable by Expressing Appreciation for Your Loved Ones.

Though divorce rate statistics in the fire service are staggering, as in any marriage, successfully navigating the hard times requires expressing appreciation for one another. This may sound simple, but expressing appreciation for your spouse has been shown to be one of the most significant preventatives of divorce or separation (Gottman, 2015).

Be Vulnerable by Discussing Couple and Family Therapy Options.

People often say things in therapy that they can't seem to say or avoid saying without a professional present. This is why it can be extremely helpful to incorporate couple therapy and family therapy into the healing process along with individual therapy to resolve issues surrounding trauma.

Chapter Seven
What Exactly is EMDR?

Due to the popularity of EMDR therapy with first responders, you may have heard of it, so I want to devote some attention to it and hopefully answer some questions you may have about it. Eye movement desensitization and reprocessing (EMDR) therapy is a type of trauma treatment that targets and reprocesses traumatic memories. A great thing about EMDR is that it tackles past and present trauma triggers but also helps you prepare for future trauma exposure, which you certainly will have if you plan on remaining a firefighter. EMDR has been shown to be extremely effective at treating critical incident traumas as well as developmental and complex trauma (Parnell, 2013).

EMDR utilizes a technique known as *bilateral stimulation* to unlock traumatic memories that are stuck, allowing the brain and nervous system to process the traumatic memory the way it processes any other memory. Bilateral stimulation accomplishes this by activating the brain and autonomic nervous system in such a way that allows adaptive information to replace traumatic information (Shapiro, 2018). Furthermore, bilateral stimulation has been shown to access the networks where trauma is stored, similar to what is supposed to take place during rapid eye movement (REM) stages of sleep (Shapiro, 2018). Basically, trauma deactivates your natural ability to process information in an helpful way (Knipe, 2019), and bilateral stimulation reactivates your natural ability to process information in a helpful way (Shapiro, 2018).

Applying bilateral stimulation during EMDR or even on its own has been shown to:

- Reduce the threat response related to traumatic events
- Reduce the level of distress when recalling a traumatic memory
- Reduce the desire to avoid thoughts, feelings, situations, and places related to traumatic events
- Activate the "rest-and-digest" mode of the parasympathetic nervous system
- Desensitize you to the intense images of a traumatic memory
- Decrease the activation in the amygdala, the brain's "smoke detector," when recalling traumatic events
- Reduce or eliminate flashbacks and nightmares (Knipe, 2019)

In summary, trauma-informed therapy, including EMDR, frees you not only from the effects of trauma but also from the negative beliefs associated with traumatic memories, as well as from the actual body sensations associated with those memories. If you decide to seek help from a mental health professional, ask them about EMDR. It's not the only solution, but it's certainly worth exploring.

Chapter Eight

It's Ultimately Up To You

"Showing Up" for Yourself in Therapy

Coming to therapy is extremely coura-geous but it is not a cure-all. Once you're there, you still have to put in the work. You have to give yourself permission to heal. You have to show up for yourself. You have to allow your-self to be vulnerable in ways that you may not initially be comfortable with or accustomed to. Therapists cannot make you heal just be-cause they have credentials. You have to lis-ten and allow the therapist to figure out how best to help you. Therapy is not one size fits all. There are standard operating procedures in therapy, but each individual needs to be ap-proached uniquely and it's up to you to assist the therapist in determining what will most benefit *you*. You also have to be willing to put in some effort between sessions. This should not be viewed as "homework" but as an opportunity to practice what you learn so that you develop new habits that produce long-term effects on your physical health.

Self-Help Tips to Implement Between Therapy Sessions

There are a number of things you can do to significantly reduce the impact of trauma on your nervous system between therapy sessions.

Any self-regulation technique that you want to use is fine. Even searching for "self-regulation techniques" online can be very helpful. The goal is to eliminate the stress response from the body by relaxing all the muscles in your body. How you choose to do this is up to you. Use whatever self-regulation techniques that work for you. The ones mentioned in this book are simply suggestions, and they can all be done in under thirty seconds.

Remember How to Breathe. We often hold our breath and take shallow breaths throughout the day without even realizing it. To combat this, practice breathing for four (4) seconds through your nose, followed by holding your breath for four (4) seconds, and then exhaling that breath through your nose for six (6) seconds—basically, 4-4-6. Breathing in and out through your nose activates your ventral vagal nerve network and reduces the activity in your sympathetic nervous system and your organ systems. Breathing through your nose also boosts your immune system. You only need to practice breathing 4-4-6 once before you start to notice a difference in how you feel physically. Make sure to breathe using your diaphragm rather than breathing from your chest or throat. Your diaphragm is a muscle, and when you constrict and release it through breathing, it makes stress or anxiety impossible.

Pelvic Floor Exercise. Pelvic floor muscles work like a trampoline at the bottom of your pelvis that support your pelvic organs. Tightening and releasing these muscles activates a complete systemic relaxation (Gentry, 2021). As a reference, these are the muscles you would use if you were to stop urinating once you've already started. These are also the muscles used when performing Kegel exercises. Practice tightening these muscles for about five (5) seconds and then releasing them for five (5) seconds. Repeat three (3) times or more if you'd like. Make sure to focus your attention on your pelvic floor muscles while doing this to avoid using the muscles in your stomach, legs, or buttocks. It's amazing how something so simple can remove the stress from your entire body in a matter of seconds.

Scanning the Body for Muscle Tension. There are over 650 skeletal muscles in your body. Odds are you are flexing some of these muscles without realizing it, even right now. Even if you scan your body for tension, you will likely miss some or you will tense them back up shortly after you release them. It is very helpful to take five (5) to ten (10) seconds to mentally scan your body to see if you notice any involuntary muscle tension. Because you literally cannot experience stress in a relaxed body (Gentry, 2021), releasing muscle tension should be one of your top priorities from now on. The good news is you can scan your body for tension and then release the tension without stopping whatever you're doing. Try it now: start from the top of your scalp, and move your attention downward, releasing any tense muscles you notice all the way down to your feet. Then do the same thing from your feet back up to your scalp. The more often you do it, the better you will get at doing it automatically. Some chronically tense muscle groups that tend to go unnoticed are muscles in the face, the jaw, the throat, the shoulders, and the pelvic floor.

Feet on the Ground... Literally. Standing or walking barefoot on the sand, grass or dirt—literally any natural ground cover—can make you feel better about yourself. There are reflex points in your feet that crave the sensation of natural elements. Not convinced? Give it a try: spend two minutes walking barefoot in the grass or on the sand, and you will be surprised at how good you feel.

Conclusion

Understanding the impact of work-related trauma you experience as a firefighter brings both challenges and benefits. It can stir up emotions that you have tried hard to keep at bay, but working through trauma will bring clarity to your life that you haven't had in a long time. It will feel like tremendous relief to have your life back so you can finally be present and deeper connected to yourself and the ones you love. Eventually, you will end up enjoying your time off-duty in a truly positive way.

Chapter Nine

RESOURCES

SIGNS OF TRAUMA QUESTIONNAIRE

ANXIETY

- Do you find it difficult to fall asleep or stay asleep while off duty?
- Do you regularly experience irritability or anger while on or off duty?
- Do you regularly experience difficulty concentrating while on or off duty?
- Do worry often?
- Do you notice yourself being more vigilant by scanning your environment and surroundings for threats or danger?
- Do you notice that you are more easily startled when you unexpectedly hear a loud noise or someone tries to get your attention?

AVOIDANCE

- Do you avoid thoughts and feelings related to a traumatic event?
- Do you avoid talking about traumatic events?
- Have you forgotten certain aspects of a traumatic event, or are they difficult to remember?
- Have you noticed you are no longer interested in things you used to enjoy?
- Have you noticed you no longer feel connected or close to important people in your life?
- Do you have difficulty experiencing your emotions or notice you feel numb?
- Do you sometimes feel that your future is bleak or that your life will be cut short?

RELIVING

- Do you have recurrent and distressing memories of a call or several calls?
- Do you have nightmares or upsetting dreams about work-related calls?

- Do you sometimes feel like a call is happening all over again, either in images, or by losing sense of time?
- Do you get extremely upset when something in the environment reminds you of a particular call?
- Does your body react to things that remind you of traumatic call?

OTHER SYMPTOMS

- Do you experience brief, abrupt or even prolonged periods of sadness, crying, or hopelessness?
- Do you find it difficult to keep up with your routine when off duty?
- Do you blame yourself for what happened on particular calls?
- Do you sometimes feel guilty about what you did or didn't do during a critical incident?
- Do you experience periods of intense anxiety associated with a particular call?
- Do you find yourself trying to keep busy all of the time while off duty?

This questionnaire was developed for use as a self-assessment of multiple key areas related to trauma and chronic stress. It is not to be used for formal diagnostic purposes. However, it is a useful tool to bring attention to potential trauma and chronic stress for further evaluation with a mental health professional.

LIFELINES AND SUPPORT

Suicide Prevention Resources

suicidepreventionlifeline.org
Suicide prevention lifeline phone number (24/7):
(800) 272 8255
workplacesuicideprevention.com

Critical Incident Stress Management and Trauma Resources

Forward-Facing Institute:
forward-facing.com
EMDR International Association:
EMDRIA.org
The Counseling Team International:
thecounselingteam.com

Premier First Responder Psychological Services (https://premier1stresponder.com)

Substance Use and Chemical Dependency Support and Resources

Thru Health – Online Intensive Outpatient (IOP) Addiction & Mental Health Care

First Responder Wellness. Addiction & Mental Health Care in Newport Beach, CA (https://www.firstresponder-wellness.com)

Alcoholics Anonymous (AA) (aa.org)

Narcotics Anonymous (NA) (na.org)

AL-ANON (al-anon.org)

Am I an Addict? NA Questionnaire (na.org)

CAGE-AID Questionnaire - World Health Organization (WHO.int)

Substance Abuse and Mental Health Services Administration (SAMHSA.gov)

Trauma-Informed Resources (Available Online)

Adverse Childhood Experiences (A.C.E) Questionnaire

Posttraumatic Checklist - PCL-5 (ptsd.va.gov)

Afterword

My hope is that this book brings a greater understanding to you regarding the traumatic effects that come with working in the fire service, that it brings some relief and normalizes your experiences, and that it motivates you to seek the right kind of assistance so that you can start living the life you want to live free from the aftermath of trauma. You can have your life back after trauma if you want it; you just have to want it enough.

When firefighters who were once clients reach out to tell me how grateful they are that their life was saved or positively changed by coming to therapy, I feel honored and grateful to have been along for even the smallest part of their journey. You deserve to allow yourself to heal.

Acknowledgements

I would like to thank all of the firefighters who have come to see me and who have been courageous enough to put in the work to get their lives back. Your stories are truly inspiring.

References

American Psychiatric Association (Ed.). (2013). *Diagnostic and statistical manual of mental disorders* (5th ed.). Arlington, Virginia: American Psychiatric Publishing.

Gentry, J.E. (2021) *Forward-facing freedom: Healing the past, transforming the present, a future on purpose.* Parker, CO: Outskirts Press.

Gerson, M.J. (2021). *Child abuse and trauma.* Westlake Village, CA: Institute of Advanced Psychological Studies.

Gottman, J., Silver, N. (2015). *The seven principles for making marriage work: A practical guide from the country's foremost relationship expert.* New York, NY: Harmony Publishing.

Greenwald, R. (2013). *Progressive counting within a phase model of trauma-informed treatment.* New York, NY: Routledge.

Knipe, J. (2019). *EMDR toolbox: Theory and treatment of complex PTSD and dissociation.* New York, NY: Springer Publishing Company.

Parnell, L. (2013). *Attachment-focused EMDR: Healing relational trauma.* New York, NY: Norton.

Shapiro, F. (2012). Getting past your past: Take control of your life with self-help techniques from EMDR therapy. New York, NY: Rodale.

Shapiro, F. (2018). *Eye movement desensitization and reprocessing (EMDR) therapy: Basic principles, protocols, & procedures* (3rd ed.). New York, NY: The Guilford Press.

Sweeton, J. (2019). *EMDR mastery course: Assessment, resourcing, and treatment techniques for trauma and anxiety.* Eau Claire, WI: Pesi.

Walker, P. (2013). *Complex PTSD: From surviving to thriving.* San Bernardino, CA: An Azure Coyote Book.

Library of Congress Control Number: 2021923421

ISBN 979-8-9853134-0-6 (hardcover)
ISBN 979-8-9853134-1-3 (paperback)
ISBN 979-8-9853134-2-0 (eBook-kindle)
ISBN 979-8-9853134-3-7 (eBook-ePub)

About the Author

Peter Salerno, Psy.D., LMFT, is a licensed psychotherapist and award- winning author residing in Southern California, who holds a doctoral degree in psychology, a master's degree in clinical psychology, and a bachelor's degree in English literature. Dr. Salerno is a trauma specialist who utilizes evidence-based, attachment-oriented approaches to promote healing and self-empowerment. He works with individuals of all ages, couples, and families in private practice. Dr. Salerno grew up in a firefighter family. His father is a retired fire captain, and his brother is a firefighter the union president of his department. Dr. Salerno is dedicated to healing those who serve and their family members.

Website: drpetersalerno.com
Email: peter@drpetersalerno.com
Instagram: @drpetersalerno

Other Titles by Peter Salerno, PsyD

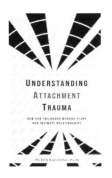

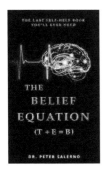

NOTES

NOTES

NOTES

NOTES

NOTES

Made in United States
Troutdale, OR
11/15/2024

24872060R00063